# What is
# weather?

Robin Johnson

Crabtree Publishing Company
www.crabtreebooks.com

**Author**
Robin Johnson

**Publishing plan research and development**
Sean Charlebois, Reagan Miller
Crabtree Publishing Company

**Editors**
Reagan Miller, Crystal Sikkens

**Proofreader**
Kathy Middleton

**Photo research**
Crystal Sikkens

**Design**
Ken Wright

**Production coordinator
and prepress technician**
Ken Wright

**Print coordinator**
Katherine Berti

**Illustrations**
Barbara Bedell: page 8
Katherine Berti: page 9

**Photographs**
Shutterstock: front cover, pages 5, 7, 11 (except top right),
  12, 16, 19 (except calendar), 20 (except calendar), 21, 22
Thinkstock: back cover, pages1, 3, 4, 6, 10, 11 (top right),
  13, 14, 15, 17, 18, 19 (calendar), 20 (calendar)

**Library and Archives Canada Cataloguing in Publication**

Johnson, Robin (Robin R.)
   What is weather? / Robin Johnson.

(Weather close-up)
Includes index.
Issued also in electronic formats.
ISBN 978-0-7787-0756-1 (bound).--ISBN 978-0-7787-0763-9 (pbk.)

   1. Weather--Juvenile literature.
I. Title.  II. Series: Weather close-up

QC981.3.J64 2012      j551.5      C2012-904367-2

**Library of Congress Cataloging-in-Publication Data**

CIP available at Library of Congress

# Crabtree Publishing Company

www.crabtreebooks.com      1-800-387-7650

Printed in Canada/102013/MA20130906

**Published in Canada**
**Crabtree Publishing**
616 Welland Ave.
St. Catharines, Ontario
L2M 5V6

**Published in the United States**
**Crabtree Publishing**
PMB 59051
350 Fifth Avenue, 59th Floor
New York, New York 10118

**Published in the United Kingdom**
**Crabtree Publishing**
Maritime House
Basin Road North, Hove
BN41 1WR

**Published in Australia**
**Crabtree Publishing**
3 Charles Street
Coburg North
VIC 3058

# Contents

# What is weather?

**Weather** is what the air and sky are like each day. Some days, the air is very cold and the sky is cloudy. Snow may fall from the clouds. You can catch snowflakes on your tongue! Other days, the air is warm and the sky is sunny. You can catch butterflies and baseballs in your back yard.

## Parts of weather

Sunshine, clouds, **wind**, water, and **temperature** are all parts of weather. Temperature is how warm or cold the air is. When the temperature is warm, water falls from the clouds as rain. When the temperature is cold, water falls as snow. Water that falls from the sky in liquid or solid form is called **precipitation**.

**What do you think?**

*What kind of precipitation is in this picture? Is it liquid or solid?*

# Weather changes

Weather changes from day to day. You can see and feel that the weather is different each day. Some days, you can see clouds moving across the sky and rain dripping down your window. Other days, you can feel cool wind on your skin and in your hair. Wind is moving air. What weather do you see and feel today?

*Weather can change quickly! A sunny picnic lunch can be canceled by a sudden rain shower.*

# What is climate?

Weather changes from day to day, but **climate** does not often change. Climate describes the usual weather **pattern** in an area. Climate can determine where people live and the crops they grow. Earth has four main climates. They are polar, temperate, dry, and tropical.

*Dry climates have very little rainfall. Temperatures are hot during the day and cold at night.*

*Temperate climates have weather that changes with the seasons.*

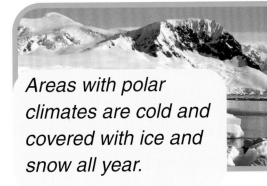

*Areas with polar climates are cold and covered with ice and snow all year.*

*Tropical climates are very hot and rainy all year long.*

# The Earth and Sun

The Sun makes weather on Earth. The Sun shines on Earth and heats the ground. The ground heats the air above it, giving us warm temperatures. The Sun gives us seasons, too. A season is a time of year with certain weather.

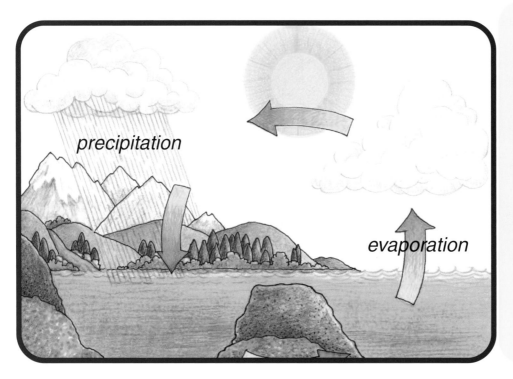

precipitation

evaporation

The Sun also heats water on Earth. The heated water **evaporates**, or turns from a liquid to a gas. The gas rises up and turns into clouds. The water then falls back to Earth as precipitation.

# Here comes the Sun

Earth travels around the Sun once each year. As Earth moves, some areas on Earth get more sunlight than others at certain times of the year. This makes our seasons. For example, in summer North America is closer to the Sun, so the days are hotter and there are more hours of sunlight.

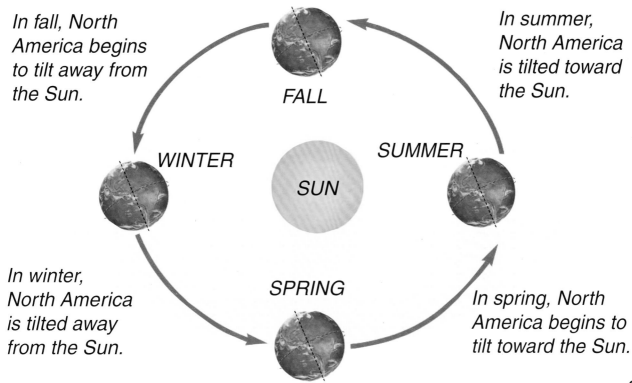

In fall, North America begins to tilt away from the Sun.

In summer, North America is tilted toward the Sun.

FALL

WINTER

SUMMER

SUN

SPRING

In winter, North America is tilted away from the Sun.

In spring, North America begins to tilt toward the Sun.

# The four seasons

Each year has four seasons in many parts of the world. They are winter, spring, summer, and fall. The weather is different in each season. Different parts of the world have seasons at different times of the year. For example, when it is winter in North America, it is summer in Australia.

The summer months in Australia are December, January, and February. So, Christmas falls in the middle of summer there.

The four seasons always change in the same pattern. Winter is the coldest season. Then the air becomes warmer in spring. Summer follows spring with hot temperatures. Then the air starts to feel cooler as fall begins. Winter starts again after fall.

What do you think?

*Which season is each of these pictures showing? How can you tell?*

# Studying the weather

Scientists that study and measure the weather are called **meteorologists**. Meteorologists keep track of the weather to see how it changes over time. They watch and **predict** what the weather will be like. To predict means to tell what will happen in the future. Meteorologists warn people when there are storms on the way.

Hurricanes are big wind storms. Th bring heavy rain and high winds tha can cause a lot of damage.

## What do you think?

Why else is it important to know what the weather will be like each day?

wind sock

rain gauge

wind vane

thermometer

## Weather tools

Meteorologists use many tools to help them predict the weather. They use **thermometers** to measure the temperature of the air. Meteorologists use wind vanes and wind socks to figure out which direction the wind is blowing. They use rain gauges to measure how much rain falls.

# Dress for the weather

This fox is dressed for the weather! It has thick fur to keep it warm in cold temperatures.

Knowing what the weather will be like helps people plan how to dress each day. When the weather is wet and rainy, you wear a raincoat and rubber boots to stay dry. When the weather is cool and windy, you wear a sweater or jacket to keep warm. How did you dress for the weather today?

14

# Play it safe!

When the weather is hot and sunny, it is important to wear sunscreen and a sunhat. You should drink a lot of water and cool off in the shade. When the weather is cold, you should dress in warm clothing. Always wear a hat to keep your head warm in cold weather.

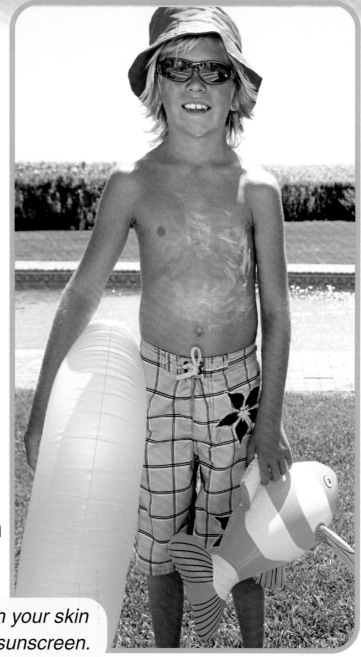

*The Sun is very hot! It can burn your skin if you do not cover up or wear sunscreen.*

# Rain or shine

Knowing what the weather will be like also helps people plan what to do each day. You can do different things in different types of weather. On sunny days, you can draw chalk pictures on the sidewalk. If it started to rain, your drawings would be washed away! Cold, snowy days are good for making snowmen. On windy days, you can fly a kite.

*This girl is splashing in puddle on a rainy spring day.*

## What do you think?

*What are some other things that you can do in different types of weather?*

16

# We need weather!

All living things need sunlight and water to stay alive. Plants need rain and sunlight to grow. Rain and snow fill the lakes and rivers. Animals use this water to drink. Water from lakes and rivers is also brought into homes through pipes. We use this water to drink, bathe, and clean our clothes and dishes.

## What do you think?

*What else do you use the water in your home for?*

# Make a weather calendar

## Materials:

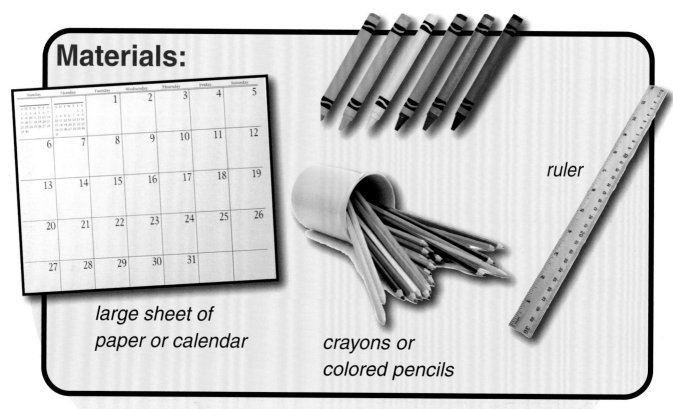

large sheet of
paper or calendar

crayons or
colored pencils

ruler

Follow these steps to make a **weather calendar**.
A weather calendar is a chart that shows the days
in a month and what the weather is like each day.

18

# What to do:

**1**. Print off a calendar from the Internet or use your crayons and ruler to draw a calendar on a blank piece of paper. Be sure to include the name of the month, days of the week, and number of days.

**2**. Once you have your calendar ready, watch the weather at the same time each day. Is it sunny or cloudy? Is it raining or snowing? It is windy or calm?

| Sunday | Monday | Tuesday | Wednesday | Thursday | Friday | Saturday |
|---|---|---|---|---|---|---|
| | | 1 | 2 | 3 | 4 | 5 |
| 6 | 7 | 8 | 9 | 10 | 11 | 12 |
| 13 | 14 | 15 | 16 | 17 | 18 | 19 |
| 20 | 21 | 22 | 23 | 24 | 25 | 26 |
| 27 | 28 | 29 | 30 | 31 | | |

**3**. Draw a small picture in each square of the calendar to show what the weather was like on that day. By doing this, you are collecting weather **data**, or information.

**4**. Use your calendar to keep track of the weather for a month or even a whole year!

# Look and learn

Use your calendar to learn about the weather. Look at the pictures on your calendar at the end of each month. What do you see? Did the weather change over time? Are there patterns in the weather? A pattern is something that repeats.

| Sunday | Monday | Tuesday | Wednesday | Thursday | Friday | Saturday |
|--------|--------|---------|-----------|----------|--------|----------|
| | | 1 | 2 | 3 | 4 | 5 |
| 6 | 7 | 8 | 9 | 10 | 11 | 12 |
| 13 | 14 | 15 | 16 | 17 | 18 | 19 |
| 20 | 21 | 22 | 23 | 24 | 25 | 26 |
| 27 | 28 | 29 | 30 | 31 | | |

# Tally it up!

Use your calendar to make a tally chart. A tally chart uses marks to keep track of how often something happens. Each tally mark in a tally chart represents one object. For example, to show three rainy days, you make three tally marks on the chart. Tally marks are grouped in sets of five.

*Look at your calendar and count the number of days for each kind of weather. Record the number beside the matching picture.*

## Tally chart

| | |
|---|---|
| ☀ | 卌 I |
| ⛅ | 卌 卌 |
| ☁ | 卌 I |
| ☁☁ | I |
| ❄☁ | III |
| ☀❄ | II |
| 🌧 | IIII |

# Reading a bar graph

You can use the data from your tally chart to create a bar graph. A bar graph is a useful tool for comparing data. The parts of a bar graph are labeled below.

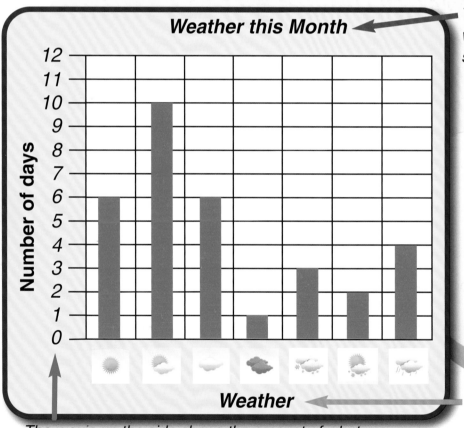

The *title* describes what the graph is showing.

**What do you think?**

Use the bar graph to answer these questions.
1. What kind of weather happened the most?
2. What kind of weather happened the least?
3. What season do you think it might be?

The *y-axis* up the side shows the amount of what the graph is measuring. The y-axis begins at 0.

The *x-axis* along the bottom shows the things being compared.

# Find out more

## Books

*Changing Seasons (Nature's Changes)* by Bobbie Kalman and Kelley MacAulay. Crabtree Publishing Company, 2005.

*Changing Weather: Storms (Nature's Changes)* by Kelley MacAulay and Bobbie Kalman. Crabtree Publishing Company, 2006.

*The Weather (Now we know about)* by Mike Goldsmith. Crabtree Publishing Company, 2009.

*What is climate? (Big Science Ideas)* by Bobbie Kalman. Crabtree Publishing Company, 2012.

## Websites

Fossweb Air and Weather Module
www.fossweb.com/modulesK-2/AirandWeather/index.html

United States Search and Rescue Task Force: Predicting Weather
www.ussartf.org/predicting_weather.htm

Weather Wiz Kids
www.weatherwizkids.com/

# Glossary

**Note:** Some boldfaced words are defined where they appear in the book.

**climate** (KLAHY-mit) noun  The weather that an area has had for a long period of time

**meteorologist** (mee-tee-uh-ROL-uh-jist) noun  A scientist who studies and measures weather

**pattern** (PAT-ern) noun  Something that repeats

**precipitation** (pri-sip-i-TEY-shuhn) noun  Water in liquid or solid form that falls from clouds

**predict** (pri-DIKT) verb  To tell what will happen before it takes place

**season** (SEE-zuhn) noun  A period of time with certain temperatures and weather

**temperature** (TEHM-per-a-chur) noun  How cold or warm the air is

**weather** (WEH-thur) noun  What the air and sky are like each day

**wind** noun  Air that blows over Earth

*A noun is a person, place, or thing. A verb is an action word that tells you what someone or something does.*

# Index